The legacies passed on
family have strongly in
edly made me what I
book brought memories of the times when wisdom
was imparted into my life. I treasure those moments
and you will too!

—Dr. Marilyn Hickey
Marilyn Hickey Ministries

Dr. Reid has done a remarkable job of illustrating
how her grandmother planted seeds of faith that
yielded amazing fruit in her own life and the lives of
her children. I found this book both encouraging and
challenging.

—Nancy Parker Brummett
Author of *Simply the Savior*
and *It Takes a Home*

As a teenager, Dr. Bernice Strand Reid was annoyed
by her grandmother's tendency to give her advice. One
day, her grandmother told Dr. Reid to put the advice
"on the shelf" and take it down when she needed it.
Looking back on her life, Dr. Reid realized just how
often she had gone to "Grandmother's shelf"; indeed,
it may be said that she depended on that shelf for
daily subsistence. Through her new book, Dr. Bernice
Strand Reid not only paints a loving portrait of the
upright woman who was her grandmother and child-
hood mentor, she also bestows on her readers some
well-chosen gifts of godly wisdom to place on their

own shelves. Heart-warming examples from Dr. Reid's life serve as poignant illustrations of her grandmother's advice, which was firmly grounded in God's Word. Readers are sure to find themselves going back again and again to *Grandmother's Shelf* to retrieve one or two or more "golden apples" of wisdom.

—DHAKSHIKE WICKREMA
LOS ANGELES, CALIFORNIA

How amazing that one Bible-believing, God-fearing, Spirit-driven grandmother could, alone, impact the lives of future generations with words of truth and wisdom gleaned from the Holy Bible! This little lady exposed God's instruction—His "love letter" for Christians—to everyone she met. Of greatest importance, her granddaughter Bernice was placed at the front of the "class" by God's own hand, as her grandmother taught life experiences and God's wisdom to her eager-to-learn student.

It was 2002 when I first became acquainted with Dr. Bernice Strand Reid while serving on her Executive Board of the National League of American Pen Women, Washington, DC. As president of a women's professional organization that boasted a membership of approximately 3,000 and had been in existence more than 100 years, Dr. Reid surprised many by refusing in any way, in any situation, to venture from the truth. When something came up that did not follow the law of man or God, her reason for choosing the correct and honest decision was, "It's the right thing to do." She became well known throughout the league for that response.

After reading this book, I now understand how the author's grandmother, God's appointed "potter," sculpted her precious granddaughter into the wonderful person she is today. I also understand how and why each of Dr. Reid's six children excelled as a professional person with high honors. Each served God and shares His love with others.

Grandmother's Shelf is a must-read for all. It leaves us with the knowledge that truth is the most valuable virtue we can possess.

—FERN MORRIS VETTER
PROFESSIONAL NURSE, JOURNALIST,
FINE ART PHOTOGRAPHER, AND FEATURE WRITER

Grandmother's *Shelf*

BERNICE REID

CREATION HOUSE
H O U S E
A STRANG COMPANY

GRANDMOTHER'S SHELF by Bernice Reid
Published by Creation House
A Strang Company
600 Rinehart Road
Lake Mary, Florida 32746
www.strangbookgroup.com

Unless otherwise noted, all Scripture quotations have been paraphrased by the author.

Design Director: Bill Johnson
Cover design by Nathan Morgan

Library of Congress Control Number: 2010937174

International Standard Book Number
Paperback version: 978-1-61638-254-4
Hardback version: 978-1-61638-260-5

First Edition

10 11 12 13 14 — 9 8 7 6 5 4 3 2 1
Printed in the United States of America

A word fitly spoken
is like apples of gold
in pictures of silver.

PROVERBS 25:11, KJV

Lives of great men all remind us,
We can make our lives sublime,
And, departing, leave behind us,
Footprints on the sands of time;

Footprints, that perhaps another,
Sailing o'er life's solemn main,
A forlorn and
shipwrecked brother,
Seeing, shall take heart again.

HENRY WADSWORTH LONGFELLOW

Dedication

- To the memory of my grandmother, Mattie Lou Murnia Blakey

- To my husband, Carlton, who has continually supported all my endeavors

- To my children and grandchildren

- To my mother, Julia S. Hinch and siblings, Julia Potter, Mildred Williams, Frances Baker, Kathryn Flagg, Anna Burrell Laws, Lewis C. and Josey Strand, Jr., Raymond Strand, William C. and Jane Strand, Elder Horace W. and Doreen Strand and all their offspring. In memory of John S. Strand and Marshall J. Strand

- To the memory of Bishop Strobhar, First Pentecostal Holy Church, Godparents Clara and Ernest Ellis

- To the memory of Elder Howard and Dorothy Spicer, and all those who had a hand in my godly upbringing

- Geneva Ellis and my Godbrother and his wife, Elder Samuel and Vernadine Ellis, and to all those who preach the gospel of Jesus Christ and the televangelists on Trinity Broadcast Network

- To my best friend of more than fifty years, Joyce Pierce, once an acting mayor of Lawnside, New Jersey, who served with me on our college newspaper and continues the friendship and support in prayerful conversations

- Jean Holmes, president, and friends from the National League of American Pen Women, Inc.

- To dear friend Fern Vetter, endorser

- To dear friend Nancy Brummett, endorser

- Especially to Mildred Cox, poet laureate, of Marmoroneck, New York, who inspired me to write the book on my grandmother and pushed me until it was done

Acknowledgments

I ACKNOWLEDGE SEVERAL INDIVIDUALS WHO have encouraged me and lent support during the creation of this book:

- My daughter, Dawn, who read the first manuscript and felt the love in it

- My eldest son, Col. Carlton Reid

- Dhakshi Wickrema, who formatted the first draft of the book

- Kate Douma, my French student and dear friend with whom I shared my grandmother's wisdom

- The publishers at Creation House, including staff members Jihan Ruano, Brenda Davis, Ann Stoner, and Virginia Maxwell

- Dr. Marilyn Hickey, who graciously endorsed my book, thereby lending her considerable credibility to it

Introduction

WHEN I WAS TEENAGER, I tired of my grandmother's constant teaching and lecturing. One day, I retorted to her, "All you do is lecture me," and to avoid hearing more, I left the house and took a long walk. On my return, she said to me in a gentle voice, "All I do is lecture you, huh? All right, if you don't think you need my advice now, then put it on the shelf and take it down when you need it." I can now say that I have gone to that "shelf" many times for her advice to help me with the challenges I face and have faced in my life. However, I am getting ahead of my story about my wise and loving grandmother. Although she has been deceased for decades, I still miss her. I am grateful for all that she gave me.

This story is about my maternal grandmother, Mattie Blakey. She was the daughter of Sallie Mae Blackwell and Mr. Murnia of Danburg, Georgia. She called herself Mattie "Meriney" but spelled it Murnia.

She married William Cleveland Blakey and had two children, Joseph and Julia, and in the 1900s the family moved to Pennsylvania.

William Cleveland Blakey

Julia, who married Lewis Corbin Strand Jr. of Upland, Pennsylvania, became my mother in February 1936. I was blessed with genetically smart parents, a wise and witty grandmother, and a caring grandfather on my maternal side, as well as outstanding paternal grandparents. My mother gave me a great deal of training and education in poetry, crafts, vocal music, and stories from a children's Bible. In my pre-kindergarten training, she took pride in preparing me for school. Mother recounts this story: Whenever I repeated the alphabet, I would say, "double Mommy" instead of "W" (that was a child's analogy of the letter).

Grandmother with my mother, Julia,
after a dinner party

My grandmother Mattie was conscious of serious study. She learned to express herself in the best grammar, diction, and tone of voice. She knew she had only a sixth grade education, one that most blacks in the South could attain in her day. Therefore, she enrolled in night school at Douglas Junior High as an adult in Chester, Pennsylvania. With her dedication, she achieved her goals so that all who met her did not know that she had migrated from Georgia, because she did not speak with the southern drawl of Georgia.

As I progressed through school, she asked me to share with her what I was learning. What I can remember of her was her tall stature, ladylike bearing, soft voice, and loving character for her son, Uncle Joe, and my mother, "Matt Jule." She passed on her love of knowledge to my mother and my uncle. Uncle Joe allowed me to use his little library of the classics for careful reading. As soon as I finished one book and put it back, I was allowed to borrow another book.

Therefore, while growing up, I spent a lot of time at my grandparents' house. First of all, I liked the treats they would give me and also enjoyed the player piano on which I could play the perforated paper rolls while pumping with my feet. I stopped at my grandparents' house nearly every day on my way home from school. I enjoyed it so much that my grandparents decided I should take piano lessons from Abby Garnet, the choir director, organist, and piano teacher who came to Chester once a week to give private instruction.

I remember skipping to that house with its smell of the old, large, dark furniture and oriental rugs, which adorned the rather old-fashioned parlor with its upright piano. It seemed a bit imposing to me as a little girl. It was the home of a kind and respected deacon and his wife, whose home served as a parsonage for our pastor (the pastor lived there part-time, as he been called to serve another congregation in New Jersey). It was a new pleasure for me to sit with a couple of other students and wait my turn.

It was a serious endeavor, but somehow I knew that this was special and practiced daily at my grandparents' house to get the encouraging comments and gold stars Mrs. Garnet put on the pieces that I played well. She was a firm but accomplished musician herself, who required good performance. I worked hard for the "excellent" comment she would write at the top of the page, but I was disappointed when she wrote, "needs improvement" and assigned those pieces again for the next week. I wanted my grandparents to be proud.

Even though she was kindhearted, my grandmother was stoic and unaffectionate, which she said came from her Indian background. I knew she loved me by her deeds and the time she spent with me. She would teach me about Indian foods, how she grew up picking cotton, and about how hard the work of hoeing cotton was. She talked to me about how people took care of themselves without doctors. People would find wild plants growing in the woods that could be used for medicinal purposes. One plant in particular was called "cure or kill." I think it was used to cure pneumonia and may have had antibiotic properties. If the concoction made from it did not cure, it may have killed the patient. I could just imagine her working in the fields and exploring the surrounding woods.

Once she prepared a cure for me of mutton tallow when I got a chest cold. I never forgot the smell of that poultice lovingly placed on my chest.

She also liked to show me how agile she was and her favorite exercise. Her favorite position was a stretch in which she would bend from the waist and place her hands flat on the floor in front of her. She could do this easily in one smooth move. I was never able to do this, even though I took hatha yoga lessons when I was in my thirties from the wife of the commanding general at Fort Bliss.

My grandparents and I became very close. My grandfather helped my family by giving my sisters and me beautiful clothes from John Wanamaker's in Philadelphia. I really appreciated this and received them with delight. I believe this is one of the reasons I developed an affinity for clothes with simplicity, modesty, and classic style.

As I grew older, I became a helper for my grandmother, learning how to run errands, especially going to the grocery store and the butcher shop, where I learned to pick the best cuts of meat. If purchases were not to her standards and expectations, I had to return them. I learned to be very selective and insisted on the best for my family.

During my high school years, I watched as my grandfather experienced declining health. He had to retire at age sixty-two, from the Sun Oil Company in Marcus Hook, where he had worked as supervisor. He was still a handsome and vigorous man. The change in his lifestyle resulted in too much time for leisure. He tried to start a little business by collecting articles in disrepair that he could restore. Social Security rules at that time did not permit a retired person to make a livelihood. He suffered a traffic accident that broke a leg and precipitated three strokes. It became apparent that my grandmother needed help caring for him, so my parents allowed me to move to my grandparents' home part-time. He became bedridden and partially paralyzed, so I helped my grandmother with nursing duties, especially helping to turn him in bed to change the linens. His condition worsened, and he was moved to the Chester-Crozier Hospital where he died after a few days.

After his death, I moved permanently to my grand-mother's home. She began teaching me life lessons in earnest. I became her constant companion, attending church with her, and she became my best friend. Reflecting on my life as a student, teacher, wife, mother, and professional, I realize that I would not have experienced the success found in all those roles without the power and force of her words of wisdom. In a recent university interview, I was asked about my life's pursuits, my family, and my interests. After describing them, the interviewer suddenly commented, "I can see the hand of God in your family running like a thread through your children's lives." I responded by saying that was due to my grandmother's loving but firm teaching. Her godly wisdom has guided me in my relationships within my own family. As a mother, I tried to preserve the dignity of my children by explaining my discipline and corporal punishments. As my children grew, I protected their dignity and privacy by not opening their mail, even though I wanted to know what was inside. Very early, children learn to communicate with each other through written notes not meant for parents. I could only pray that they maintained good associations. This has carried over to my son-in-law and my daughters-in-law. I do not discuss them to each other, and I never compare them. I permit them to share good news and commentary on issues with each other.

Adherence to grandmother's instructions and passing them on to my family has given my children great success. Obedience to the Word of God guarantees reward. Although not perfect, I would not change anything except for the time I took a detour and left the righteous path. I am so glad that I repented, asked for forgiveness, and received God's mercy and grace. The Lord restored me so I could enjoy the life He had planned for me. I had accepted the Lord at three years of age, and I recommitted my life at ages twelve and twenty-two, as my understanding of salvation grew. In an act of faith, my grandmother accompanied me in prayer at the altar when I made confession.

Grandmother's words of wisdom came from practical experience and the Bible. She was a committed Christian. She viewed all of life through the prism of salvation, guidance of the Holy Spirit and the dictates of the Word of God. In plain language and sometimes in her own creative pithy sayings, she would explain God's will for all in the world. She covered every aspect of living, from the cradle to the grave. She also shared how she came to know the Lord. A traditional Baptist when she and her husband moved from the South, she visited a Pentecostal church to which they had been invited by her brother and sister-in-law to join them for free entertainment. My grandmother's brother, Tommy, and his wife, Rozelle, had preceded them to Pennsylvania and told them of the unusual congregation they had visited. They were going there to laugh. On arrival, they could not believe the demonstration of fervor the members felt through shouting, singing, clapping hands, praising the Lord, and their individual testimonies of being sanctified and filled with the Holy Ghost. After hearing the message of the baptism in the Holy Ghost and sanctification on another visit, my grandmother said her pride took a fall, she stopped laughing, and she "slipped in" so she said in often-repeated testimony. She gained a new relationship with Jesus Christ and the power to live a sanctified life. Subsequently, both couples joined the optimistic Pentecostal congregation. Interestingly, my paternal grandparents, who provided their home as a meeting place to the former street minister and pastor, Nathaniel Strobhar and his growing number of followers, established the church. My paternal grandfather was a builder. His name is included in the cornerstone of the first building the church acquired on Abbott Street. Rev. Strobhar's ministry began after the pastor's calling to the ministry in the Azusa Street Revival in California, where the outpouring of the Holy Spirit is chronicled in the late nineteenth century. He had taken the Gospel to street corners in Chester, Pennsylvania, while his friends, Rev. and Mrs. James Cunningham, served in the Philadelphia area as Church of the Nazarene members. His preaching attracted many who accepted Christ with life-changing results. They received the challenge to live holy lives through the baptism of the Holy Spirit with evidence of speaking in tongues.

Elder W. N. Strobhar
District Elder of New Jersey

I received benefits of the effects of my grandmother's Christian growth as I grew up. She prayed at least three times a day, dedicating the time to the Lord. I remember her praying: "Let the words of my mouth be acceptable in Thy sight, O Lord, my strength and my Redeemer." She modeled this for me, and now I include this in my prayers.

The following lessons and remonstrations constitute my grandmother's advice to me. She educated me about proper behavior, relationships with neighbors, respect for people in general, fellow Christians in the house of God, business people, husbands and wives, and close family relations. She also taught me about modest and proper attire, communication and expressing oneself, courtship, knowing Jesus as healer, and reluctance to judge others. For all of these lessons, there were instructions in the Holy Bible, especially in Proverbs. Her words to me have been proven to be like "apples of gold in pitchers of silver" (see Prov. 25:11).

Grandmother

TRUSTING IN GOD

Whenever things seemed to go differently in life than I expected and my plans to get a job as a secretary or go to college seemed impossible, my grandmother remained calm and steady. She trusted God to bring everything and every circumstance to a good conclusion. She would say, "You needn't question Him. He knows what He is doing." The Word: "Trust in Him with all your heart and lean not on your own understanding. In all your ways acknowledge Him and He will direct your path"; or He will make your paths straight; or in another translation, He will give you success (see Prov. 3:5–6).

On Behavior

She taught good nutrition and cautioned against gluttony and a poor diet. One who does that is "digging his grave with his teeth."

She taught early rising with this rhyme: "Sluggards sleep; while others plow deep." That would get a "sleepyhead" up, although I had practiced piano too late into the night, and I had to get to school. Complaining a little, I would get up because I hated that rhyme. It was very effective (Prov. 6:10–11; 19:15; 20:4).

On Gossip

No tale bearing (gossip). God hates gossip (Rom. 1:28–32; 2 Cor. 12:20; 1 Tim. 5:13). Personally, she claimed that gossip smelled like garbage and made her stomach hurt (Prov. 18:8). She said that to a lady (the church secretary) who came to bring tales about another member of the church in my presence. She prefaced her remarks to that lady by saying, "Oh, they picked poor Robin clean, did they! I want to know: Were you there? How do you know?"

I watched with sympathy as that lady, with as much dignity as she could muster, left the living room and then the house. I believe she never returned to visit, and after that, we saw her only in church.

STIRRING IN OLD MESS

The above reminds me of another admonition, "Gossip and much discussion is unprofitable." That is what Grandmother also called "stirring in an old mess." It brings anxiety for a problem that has ended or already solved. It brings up old wounded feelings and restores an unpleasant situation again. That is a waste of time and gives place for Satan to work. If someone needs forgiveness, the best recourse is to grant that, followed by the need to forget the offense.

Further, she cautioned against rehearsing old slights and transgressions. It is the glory of a man to overlook transgressions (Prov. 19:11).

On Labor and Industry

"Whatever your hands find to do, do it with your might" (Eccles. 9:10). This is the best way to determine how to spend time doing worthwhile pursuits. I have used this approach in studying, taking care of my family of six, teaching school, learning music, art, cooking, doing philanthropic activities, being a housewife and military spouse, being a true friend, church worker, choir director, accompanist for two chapels, and ambassador to other countries while chaperoning exchange students and doing study abroad. Another version says, "Do your best." That is what you'll get from it, satisfaction and rewards that grow (Eccles. 9:10).

Since the age of seven, I always wanted to be an artist. The itinerant art teacher who came to our elementary school did not encourage me. I tried to get her attention, but she seemed to pay no attention. In God's own timing, that wish was fulfilled. God gave me the desire of my heart thirty-six years later. Like Grandmother emphasized, God will give you the desires of your heart, when you walk uprightly before Him. It is His good pleasure to give good gifts to His children.

ON TALKING

Grandmother taught lessons on being careful about talking too much. She often said that I should limit what I say in conversation, be direct, and forthright. She did not tolerate a lot of "jawing." That was what she called excessive talking. "Let your yea be yea, and your nay be nay. Anything more than that is in danger of judgment" (Matt. 5:37). "Be careful what you say and protect your life. A careless talker destroys himself" (Prov. 13:3). "A soft answer turns away wrath" (Prov. 15:1). "Smart people think before they answer. Evil people have a quick reply, but it causes trouble" (Prov. 15:29). "The smart person says very little and one with understanding stays calm. Even fools seem to be wise if they keep quiet" (Prov. 17:27–28). She often told me, "You should hold some of what you think." In sum, Mattie taught that self-control and discipline should control speech. "The tongue is the most unruly member of the body. It can set the course of hell on fire. It is like the rudder of the ship, which controls the body and its direction" (James 3:1–12).

This was not always easy because I come from a family that practiced verbal defense techniques like lawyers. We did not want anyone to get the best of us in perceived slights or to take advantage of us since we were a large family with limited resources. However, "holding my peace" and letting the Lord fight my battles was always the best strategy in fighting life's battles.

She taught me to be faithful in everything, even in small things. Her favorite verse on this subject was: "It's the little foxes that spoil the vine." She taught that it is little things that may spoil efforts in our lives. She believed in self-control, self-discipline, and exemplary decorum. Even when my grandmother was suffering from Alzheimer's and living in a convalescent home, she commented to me about the ridiculousness of another patient's lack of control with her constant screaming of profanity in the adjoining room. Grandmother suffered her own declining state of health with dignity.

She continued to demonstrate to me this axiom, "Whatever state you find yourself in, therewith be content" (Phil. 4:11). She illustrated this contentment for me on my visit to her three months before her death. At that point, she did not recognize me, as her disease had progressed. She told me I was a nice lady. If that was true, she helped to develop that "lady."

RELATIONSHIPS WITH NEIGHBORS

Grandmother did not believe in visiting our neighbors often. She was cordial and friendly but did not spend a lot of time in their houses. I rarely, if ever, saw the inside of our neighbors' homes and do not remember their décor and furnishings. We spent a little time on their porches if there was a need to convey a message or lend help. However, she taught that "howdy!" belonged to everyone and taught me to say, "How are you?" when greeting everyone we met. Beyond that, we were to mind our own business. I do not remember even borrowing a cup of sugar or anything else from the neighbors. She believed this: "Neither a borrower nor a lender be, for borrowing dulls the edge of husbandry." My teachers in elementary school also reinforced this lesson. Proverbs says, "Don't go to your neighbor's house, too much; too much of you will make him hate you." Another phrase she taught me that helped came from Romans, "If it be possible, as much as lieth in you, live peaceably with all men" (Rom. 12:18).

The most impressive warning she gave me was accompanied by a tragic story. At one time, a little girl I knew and with whom I went to school, became the victim of a fight between a man and wife whose home she was visiting with her mother. As the mother and the daughter approached the door of the quarreling neighbors, the wife was in the midst of hurling lye. It missed the husband, but the six-year-old was hit in the face with the acid. The child suffered a badly disfigured face with which she grew up. I often thought it was a horrible blow since everything else on her body developed in such beauty. Except for her face, she had a perfect silhouette.

I also saw this played out in my young adult years. A man who tried to break up an altercation between an officer's wife and her husband was accidentally shot to death. The bullet was intended for the husband, but because he was a friend of the husband and frequent visitor to the home, he could not avoid the tempest.

THE LAW IS FOR LAWBREAKERS

Grandmother did not have much sympathy for those that ran afoul of the law. She felt that people should lead circumspect lives with no equivocation. She wanted me to understand this and not be surprised when someone was caught not obeying the laws of the land. The verse that addressed this is found in 1 Timothy 5:10. In this book we are warned not to take part in the sins of others. In her words, "Don't hold the coat!" She emphasized that we should not turn a blind eye to things that were involved in wrongdoing.

ON COURTSHIP AND MARRIAGE

Grandmother wanted her other granddaughters and me to be selective with the young men we dated. One of her rules was: Don't kiss boys because that leads to something else. She did not explain what something else would be. Until I was twenty-one, I followed that mandate. Although I dated several nice young men, I kissed only one. He is my husband today after fifty-two years of marriage. Observing that one parameter probably saved me from many unknowns. After six children, I can define the "something else." In the right timing, it is something sacred and magnificent in the joy of procreation with all its attendant responsibilities of nurturing.

Another lesson she taught was to be sure to check on the status of young men whom we met. One day sitting on the porch, I heard her inquire of one of my siblings, "Is he yours or somebody else's?" She was very direct.

I also wanted to say these things to my children and grandchildren that she had said to me. I got just whom I wanted. She respected Granddaddy, and he respected her. She is the only woman I know who had two full-length fur coats in her day. I often wondered how he did that for her, especially since they had survived the Great Depression. He was certainly proud of her. He would not let her work outside of the home. Once, he appeared at the front door of the house where she had taken "day work" to request that my grandmother come with him. The woman of the house told my grandfather that she was busy ironing in the basement. He told her employer that he had come for her and that she had to leave then.

After my grandmother was called from the basement, she grabbed her purse and said goodbye. On the way home, Granddaddy told her that she was never to do that again. The story she told me conveyed what he thought of her. Also, he demanded the highest respect for her, and that went for me, too. Once when I talked back to her, he showed me that he could get angry with me. That was something I rarely experienced and then only once and never again! On that occasion, I ran home to my mother as fast as possible.

Part of the reason for that respect was the way she treated Grandfather. This lesson she passed on to me. When he came home from work, she had wonderfully cooked meals for him. I learned to cook from her. She said, "Give your husband the best meals that you can prepare. If you make a mistake and burn something, don't serve it." In the meantime, she showed me how to salvage scorched food. She told me to place the bottom of a pan quickly in a shallow layer of cold water run into a sink. The physics of that action pulled the burned taste from the food. Then one could spoon the unburned food from the pan or pot. This remaining food would not have any of the scorched taste. This technique aided me a few times in salvaging a forgotten dish on the stove.

Her instructions have helped to keep things steady when life's difficulties arise. Our marriage has certainly survived much through the births of six children, many changes of address on three continents in military life, my husband's tour of duty during the Vietnam War, retirement, and catastrophic illness. The Word of God she taught to me and my continued study of it has supported my family and maintained equilibrium. God has never failed me. He has kept His promises to me even though I was a backslider my senior year in college. As the Word says, Jesus is married to the backslider. He illustrates this through the story of the prodigal son. I can say like she said, "I got just whom I wanted."

CHILDREN OF BELIEVERS

My grandmother told me that the children of believers are marked. They have a special covering through the prayers to God for them. This was for two reasons. The prayers of believers for their children were requests for their salvation, and the second reason was their requests to guard their children from falling into dangerous and sinful temptations.

In fact, I experienced this protection when I worked in Atlantic City, between my sophomore and junior years in college. I had talked my grandmother into allowing me to leave Chester to earn money for college by serving as a nanny at the Atlantic seashore. I was to be joined by my valued schoolmate of my high school years who wanted to work there, too. As much as she could, my grandmother wanted to protect me. She would not let me go until she asked my Uncle Joe to drive us together to meet and interview the family for whom I would be working. After approval, she left me with my future employers. Both my friend and I worked that summer not far from each other. Our days off were Wednesdays, which we happily spent walking on the boardwalk in Atlantic City, taking in all the sights, smelling the aromas of food from culturally diverse restaurants, eating cotton candy, and watching the horse diving with a person his back into a vessel filled with water. That was one of the main attractions.

We also helped a family friend who owned and ran a boarding house nearby called Sonoma's Boarding House. The owner was the daughter of longtime neighbors and aunt of the blind girlfriend with whom I spent many days conversing over the backyard fence. She was friendly and always grateful for the free help my friend and I gave her. It distracted us from the everyday tasks of nanny care.

Although I had felt safe doing chambermaid chores, it was not necessarily safe for young women in that vacation and resort town. Once, while I was making a bed, a young man came up surreptitiously behind me. He threw me down on the bed and attempted to take advantage of me. A battle ensued. I fought my way to freedom. After the incident, I found my friend in another part of the motel. We told Aunt Sonoma goodbye and left. God was with me then. He was my Shield and Buckler.

We thought that everything was all fun, and we enjoyed the freedom of making our own money and decisions at age twenty-one. One evening, we finished our free time and returned for home. However, I did not go to the home of my employer because I was off the next day. Instead, I decided go to Aunt Sonoma's house. On the way there, I noticed two men following me. I intuited that this was not a good situation, so I decided to leave the sidewalk and cross to the middle of the wide boulevard street and walk there since there was no oncoming traffic to the Boardwalk that time of night, but the men kept following. As I approached the main cross street, I saw a young man walking along the sidewalk in the direction I wanted to go. I surmised he was another college student who had come to Atlantic City to work. He looked tall, strong, clean-cut, and resolute. In a flash of insight, I asked him if he would walk with me and act as though he was my friend. Wonder of wonders! He did, and he made sure that I reached my destination unharmed. When we arrived at Aunt Sonoma's house, we sat on her porch and talked. He was a pre-med student who had been accepted to Hahneman Institute in Philadelphia but had received induction papers to go into the army. We made fast friends and several days later, we went to see the *Eddy Duchin Story* at a local movie. He was always polite and respectful. He was my angel on assignment. Only God knows what those two men had planned to do.

If I had a fault, it was one that led to trouble: curiosity. That same summer, I wanted to go and visit a nightclub. Several students and I planned to go. Since

I did not drink alcohol, my friends convinced me that I did not have to drink. They told me I could have a Virgin Mary. I was told that it was a nonalcoholic drink. As we entered the club, I was turned away, but not before I adjusted my eyes to peer inside the darkened room. The irony of the situation was that I was the only one in the group who was twenty-one. We left after I was refused entrance. I believe that was God's protection preserving my innocence. Grandmother was right. I had "the mark" on me. I know now it is a covering that announces to Satan, "Back off, this child is anointed."

ON JUDGING

Grandmother was adamant about not judging others. She said that she had no hell to put them in or heaven to send them to. She said that people would be judged by their fruits. Further, we should be careful to walk soberly before the Lord ourselves. That would not leave room for making assessments of other Christians or other people. That is best left up to God.

In other words, she did not place herself in the role of a judge since she could not exact penance or give rewards.

BUSTED BY THE HOLY SPIRIT

During my senior year in college, I thought I would try something that many seemed to enjoy in college. After all, it was something my father had done habitually. He was the only person allowed to smoke in my home, though my mother hated the habit. Cigarette companies visited the college periodically to bring samples that they would distribute to students. In fact, they had representatives among the students who let the campus know when they were coming. Students would gather in excitement to get their share of the free cigarettes. Since I did not smoke, some students came and asked for my share so they could have mine as well. At first, I would not take the samples, but eventually I did so to please my dormitory mates.

Then one day, a couple of my friends convinced me to try one. After much huffing and puffing, I learned to tolerate one. However, I did not master the habit, because I could not inhale properly. The roommates knew I could not because of the long red end I left on the cigarette. Eventually, I practiced it. Not being near home, but at least 500 miles away, I thought no one would know. However, when I came home after graduation, my grandmother told me that the Holy

Spirit had told her I was smoking. I was surprised, but I did not admit to it.

That was truly a wonderful gift to me. I was ashamed of spoiling my body, "the temple of the Holy Spirit." Had I not been found out, I might have become hopelessly addicted and suffered the consequences in later years, as did my father. Not smoking did not stop me from trying it in the future because I bought into the lie that it was sociable. Thank God that He cared so much for me that He exposed this deception, and I asked for forgiveness.

ON DISCERNMENT

One of my grandmother's axioms was concerned with being careful of people with hidden motives. She believed in allowing the Holy Spirit, who is the judge of all things, to lead and guide in interacting with people. The Holy Spirit, with its gentle promptings and messages (thoughts), would warn, advise, and assist. I remember her saying about one person, "I saw him when he first drove up," meaning she perceived a hidden agenda in that person. That also helped her to know how to pray for people who came to her for help. Additionally, she told me to seek the Holy Spirit to bring things to remembrance for lost objects or forgotten actions, as well.

One day in an important time of decision, I experienced this leading of the Holy Spirit. I received guidance in a gentle thought to act on a certain problem. It was concerning money that I should not spend when I was the president of a nonprofit organization. I had been told that I could spend the interest on a bequest we were granted. One day as I was walking to my office, a gentle voice in my head told me, "Don't touch the interest." I had no idea that a court action was taking place hundreds of miles away and subsequent court action would request the return of the money, along with the interest. The principal amount had been awarded in error. Obedience to the voice ultimately saved our organization the original award, interest, penalties, and court costs. It also saved my reputation and tenure in office.

During the parenting of my children, I was assisted by the gentle promptings of the Holy Spirit whenever my husband and I had to leave them. Most of the time, we left for social events and receptions, commanded by the leaders of my husband's military posts. We did not enjoy leaving them in the hands of babysitters and were selective of the ones we employed. Most of the time, we tried to employ sitters who were adult—the grandmotherly type. In spite of that, I was attuned to the Spirit of the Lord. Many times when I felt that we should return home before an event ended, an incident would have taken place at home that needed my attention. My husband learned to trust me when I said we had to leave. We would get there just in time to give first aid for a minor injury or to take care of an unforeseen problem.

"FLIM-FLAM" MAN

This theme on Grandmother's advice is being wise and not becoming a victim of get-rich-quick money schemes that are pushed, especially during hard times. My grandmother told me that during the Great Depression, people like the "Flim–Flam" man would trick people into giving away their life savings. With promises of doubling or tripling their money, the trickster would present a plan for them to take money from their banks to trade for money in a suitcase. The trickster would show them money in the top layer of the suitcase that contained thousands of dollars. Under the top layers, was newsprint cut to the size of the money. In exchange for their legitimate dollars, they would take the suitcase. Then they were "flim-flammed." My grandfather was a victim, so she told this story dispassionately but pointedly. It is a warning to people who want to multiply wealth in a fast and easy way (Prov. 23:5–6). People who look at their riches will find that their wealth will sprout wings like an eagle and fly away.

ON ENVY AND JEALOUSY

I can barely remember having thoughts of envy or jealousy. I embraced this lesson from Grandmother. "God would not give you anything but what He has planned for you. He would not give someone else your gifts (1 Pet. 2:1–2). It is not difficult to celebrate the good achievements of others whether it is in riches or talents. One also can appreciate and celebrate what God has endowed to others.

It is His good pleasure to give his children good gifts. As Jesus said, if someone asks his father for bread, the father would not give him a stone. How much more will your Father in heaven give His children good gifts? My mother has said that I always felt that I had the best. Whatever grade I was in school, it was the best. I had the best teachers and the best books, which I brought home from school every day, whether I had homework or not. I wanted to show them off. This attitude covers everything about my life: my family, my home, and what God has given me.

GAINING WEALTH

Wisdom purports that to get wealth and great gain, one must give. The Bible says to give in the morning to this, in the evening to another thing. One does not know what shall be prosperous. Cast your bread upon the waters; it shall return on many waves. The Heavenly Father knows of what we have need, and He shall supply all our needs according to His riches in glory. In God's economy, giving is the stimulus for the Holy Spirit to give gain to His children.

This giving includes finances, time, and talents in service to the Lord and mankind. He multiplies all efforts and pecuniary gifts and other gifts that are given.

SERVING THE LORD IN THE HOME CHURCH

Even today I remember the joy I felt in being able to serve the Lord in my church, First Pentecostal Holy Church. I taught Sunday school, attended Young People's Holy Association, and assisted a wonderful missionary in an organization called the Sunshine Band, designed to reach the children of the church members and the surrounding community. This experience gave me insight into instructing young people and prepared me with approaches that I use today, along with godly wisdom. Having studied piano since the age of six, I started two choirs, one for the children of the Sunshine Band and the other for high school students. In time, I found myself playing for the church, other churches, and community events.

GAINING GODLINESS WITH WEALTH

Gaining godliness with wealth brings happiness and contentment. God adds no sorrow to it. In whatever state you find yourself, therewith be content. Whether one possesses more than he needs, or has just enough for subsistence, one should covet contentment above all.

RELATIONSHIPS WITH YOUR FELLOW MAN

The respect Grandmother taught me to have for others, the modesty in speech and dress, self-discipline, and etiquette, gained me success as a worker in my church, high school, apprentice secretary to a nonprofit executive, college student, military wife, mother, and mother-in-law. My training opened doors to great opportunities for me, of which I could not have known anything beforehand.

In an apprentice program for commercial secretarial students, I was recommended by my business teachers to work for a nonprofit executive in a civic and community organization. I had hoped to work for a lawyer. The nonprofit organization was not able to afford the stipend I was to receive. Because of the philanthropic purposes of the organization and the dedication of the director, I decided to stay and give the position my all. It turned out that this woman was related to a college president. She told him about me, and that contact led to the position of a student labor clerk in his office. After talking to my high school counselor about the college that he highly recommended, I decided to go there. Without the requisite funds, but faith in the Lord and my training, I believed that I could work my way through college. Because I could not find a lucrative position the summer after graduation from high school, that was the only option open to me. That decision to work there gave me a new life with different goals. During the first semester, the Dean of Women selected me to serve on the Women's Senate. The members of that group were to serve the college as hostesses for meetings and receptions. I was surprised and pleased.

One of the roles I was privileged to play was that of military wife to my husband. After some time observing other senior officers' wives and reading the book *Army Wife*, I complied with the first request I received to chair the telephone tree for the battalion wives. Although it was a low job on the totem pole, it turned out to be an important one. It helped me to become acquainted with all of the officers' wives in the unit and served the commander's wife. Proverbs 27:18 says, "One who takes care of a master (and Grandmother added all those who have rule over you) will be honored."

In sum, I was glad to assist my husband in a proper way and to represent him in conduct and in dress. In the course of our lives, I was elected to two Officers' Wives Clubs as board member and officer, and as the chairman for thirty-five welfare projects in the Canal Zone. One of the projects included visiting and celebrating the birthdays of the inmates of the oldest continuing leprosarium in the western hemisphere. It was an opportunity to see first-hand the ravages of the disease that was referenced in the Bible, which necessitated quarantine from the rest of society.

Because of the condition of the inmates, I had to make a decision about publicizing the benevolent activities of the Officers Wives' Club in Panama. While I conducted the administration of the welfare projects, men from the Public Information Office would accompany me on special events. At first, I was unaware of the publicity that would be generated and that the efforts of my committee would appear in the Panamanian news the next day. When I did learn of this, I chose not to include pictures of monthly celebrations with the lepers. That decision generated a threat to my chairmanship.

My sub-chairman, who asked to run that project, scheduled public information to take photographs at the leprosarium. When I asked to cancel the photography, she resigned angrily. She was the wife of an up-and-coming battalion commander. She also had influence over the wives of officers under her husband's command. The worst of the incident was that she soured my relationship with the medical staff of the leprosarium somehow, and she devised another way to get publicity. She forbade the wives on my committee to continue and asked them to resign with her. One of my neighbors and a fellow Christian apologized for having to leave. I told her not to worry, and in a prophecy that came to me in a flash of insight and to my tongue, I told her that she would one day be the battalion commander's wife.

I can say that God has a sense of humor when solving problems and exonerating His children, or at least I think so. The commander's wife took two wives to the Leprosarium one evening to sing for the inmates and the staff. Sure enough there was publicity.

Her photograph, along with those of her attendants, appeared next day under a misplaced caption. It read, "Prostitutes Arrested at Bar." On the opposite page, the three prostitutes' photographs appeared under the caption, "Three Officers Wives Sing at Leprosarium in an Evening Event." I did not see the newspaper until I went to the monthly Officers Wives' Club, where women were giggling and discussing the articles, which they happily showed me. I laughed too, but was glad that I had done nothing and could not have done anything to bring this "come-uppance."

The prophecy did come true. The commander lost his battalion in the jungle during worldwide practice maneuvers, and he was relieved on the spot. The woman to whom I had prophesied became the battalion commander's wife that day. Her husband, the executive officer, was promoted to battalion commander. Again, I had no knowledge of that until I went to another scheduled meeting.

HE WILL HOLD ME FAST

My grandmother used to sing the song, "He Will Hold Me Fast," all the time. I remember it was part of a collection from the *Gospel Pearls Book*, used as an early hymnal in our church. Grandmother and Granddaddy both sang in the choir, and I looked forward to the times this song was sung. It would make grandmother happy. Her lilting mezzo-soprano would also fill the home with the song that sometimes preceded her "word of prayer." I think this song helped to center her and keep her grounded. The hymn came to me later in my life as an adult working on the welfare projects. The powerful words are: *When I fear my faith would fail, Christ will hold me fast. When the Tempter would prevail, Christ will hold me fast. He will hold me fast, He will hold me fast; for my Saviour loves me so-oh; He will hold me fast.* (Praise the Lord.)

The project that kept my committee and me the busiest was providing a feeding program and English instruction class. We did this for the children of a Panamanian elementary school called Fe y Alegria. These children lived in the cardboard shack village located between two military locations of Amador and Curundu. The children came to school without proper nourishment, so we provided a wholesome breakfast of oatmeal and chocolate milk.

To accomplish this, I was granted special permission from the military government office to buy foodstuffs from the commissary. I decided to go shopping on alternate days when I was not doing personal shopping. This way I could keep the receipts for the program separate from my household groceries.

On one particular day, an artist friend and I were invited to view an art exhibition of the works of my portrait teacher, who was having a one-man show in downtown Panama. We were following my other art teacher's car in my station wagon, which contained the groceries that I had purchased the day before. My teacher passed through the guard gate of the post normally without incident. However, I was halted after approximately 600 feet by an unfamiliar green car parked outside of the gate. Two men in tan shirts and green trousers occupied the vehicle. After I stopped, one of the men jumped out from the car and came to the driver's side of my station wagon. Knowing that they were not American officials, I instinctively knew I should obey anyway. One of the men signaled me to roll down my window.

In the rear-view mirror of my teacher's car, she saw that we were not following her, so she stopped and waited a few minutes, knowing much more about the men who had detained me. They were investigative agents that were compared to the American CIA. Not being a native speaker of Spanish, I caught only a few words that he said. I did know enough to realize he was calling me a "contrabandista." My friend jumped from the car, ran back to the guard gate, and reported to the guard that we were being arrested.

In my rear-view mirror, I could see just my friend and no military guard through the guardhouse window. The sentry had knelt down to call the military headquarters. My teacher turned around to come see what she could do to help, since she was a native Spanish speaker and married to a Spanish-American sergeant in the U.S. Air Force and had lived in Panama for many years. She was very respectful as she addressed the men and told them what we were doing.

Afterwards, one of the men ordered me to get out of the car. I told him, "No hablo Español." I knew that I could not defend myself in Spanish, although I had one year in college and one course taught by the Civil Affairs Office in order to work as the Welfare Projects Chairman.

Gesturing, one of the men told me to roll down the rear window. I did, and he tore through the bags of cereal, flour, and powdered cocoa. In the meantime, I lowered my head to the steering wheel and said a short humble prayer: "Jesus, You're going to have to get me out of this one." As I finished the prayer, the men waved me on. As soon as my friend returned to the car, my instructor and I continued our trip to Balboa, downtown Panama. We could not help noticing a few armed soldiers who were posted along our route. When we finally arrived at the gallery, my professor asked us what happened, as we had been slated for a private showing.

Continuing our trip to the gallery took fortitude. I felt like going back to my quarters on the post, recalling the stories I had heard of missionaries and politicos being abducted and disappearing into the jungle. I recall the hesitation I had felt at this point, in taking the welfare projects chairmanship, because I had six children and one was still a baby. In first answer to the request, I told the executive officer's wife of Fort Amador that I could not do it because "I have six children." She replied, "Oh, I thought you had seven."

I called my husband who was in Washington, D.C., for a conference on budgeting. He was sent from the Comptroller's Office, a position he held at Fort Bliss prior to our moving to Panama. When he answered the phone, I said to him that he would not believe what they wanted me to do! I'm sure you don't want me to take over thirty-five welfare projects in Panama. That means I would be traveling the whole isthmus from the Pacific to the Atlantic. He replied that it was up to me.

Unsatisfied with his answer, I hung up after we had a conversation on how things were going on his trip. I considered why I was hesitating. I knew it was because of *fear*. Recalling a *Reader's Digest* story I had presented to my eighth-grade reading class in Mt. Holly, New Jersey, I sat and contemplated. The story was titled, "Face Your Fears." The message was that nothing was as bad as it seemed, if we would face it. Then the Word of God came to me. "The Lord did not give us a spirit of fear, but of love and a sound mind" (2 Tim. 1:7).

Settling down, I knew that I would say yes to the offer. So here I was, facing my fear.

What I feared did not really transpire. I was not arrested. I viewed the exhibition and returned home safe and sound. A delayed reaction came that night when I tried to go to sleep. My legs felt numb for a while. That was the least of my concerns. The Lord had blessed me to be back in my home with my family and not in a cell in a foreign country, waiting to see if the American embassy would be contacted. Jesus "held me fast."

The following evening, my husband and I attended an officers' and wives' party on post. People still asked me about the incident and how I got out of it. The most memorable questioner claimed to be an atheist. I told him that I had prayed a simple prayer and the Lord answered. He replied, "He should have, because you were doing His work." Hmm. I thought he was an atheist.

It turned out that I was not the only one concerned. I went to the local television station to promote one of the projects. Before I could get started, the host asked me about the incident, which by then was the talk of the latest incident with the totalitarian Panamanian government. I was told by a next-door neighbor, a lawyer, that the incident became part of the Panama Canal negotiations, along with the former stories of other arrests of missionaries.

My story ended well. After the detention, the Panamanian government offered my committee and me an apology and a cruise on a navy gunboat to the surrounding islands of Panama. It was a beautiful trip. I was able to take McGuffey readers to children who had no books and no building but were conducting some rudimentary scientific experiments with only what was available in nature. It was impressive.

While my husband served in Vietnam, I led a city and county effort in Willingboro, New Jersey, to collect school supplies and clothing for women, men, and children for the worn-torn village where my husband served. I was assisted by the Key Club, sponsored by Kiwanis.

This effort turned out to have more obstacles than I

had anticipated. The big question was how we would get the thousands of pounds of supplies we collected to the village in Vietnam. The supplies had to be sorted according to certain regulations, placed in cartons, crated, and transported to the docks in New York. We had to find someone to sponsor the shipment. That turned out to be the Catholic Relief Charities.

We were blessed in my neighborhood because we had a truck driver whose family was very friendly to mine. He volunteered to deliver the shipment to New York and observe its placement on a ship bound for Vietnam. The amazing thing that happened regarding the shipment was that it actually arrived at the village. Many things that had been shipped by others were confiscated by black market agents and sold in the docks of Saigon. A returning officer, who was present when it arrived, looked for my husband when he came home and told us about the shipment's arrival. It was providential that he was an officer who had served my husband as an executive officer in New Jersey. That news came two years before we heard of the success. That endeavor eventually led to my becoming a member of Art Linkletter's Military Wife of the Year program in 1972.

BE AVAILABLE TO GOD

I had often wondered after the success of that project how I could do something for Catholic Relief Charities. My opportunity came when I was operating a small Christian school that I had founded called Trinity Lyceum. At that time it was housed in the building of a charismatic church. It offered an accelerated Christian education, supplemented by courses in French and German. The school was advertised in the local newspaper. The ad attracted an executive of the local organization of the Catholic Relief Charities organization in Fort Worth, Texas.

As the Lord would have it, this young executive came to my office with a pretty young woman who seemed tense and wary. The trembling of her lips made me feel empathetic. The man asked if I was looking for a language teacher or needed someone to help. He told me that the woman was working for an airline stewardess who had arranged for her to come to America from Germany to watch her four children and to teach her and her family German. However, this woman, a refugee from Bosnia, was finding the job formidable and very stressful. She needed to find another position so that she could find some contentment.

She spoke hardly any English, so the man spoke for

her. He told me that she could help teach German. He told me that it was important for her to leave her job and find another position. He felt that working for me was what she needed since we could communicate. As soon as he told me that he was from Catholic Relief Charities, I knew this was finally a chance to do something for them.

After a short interview, I hired her though I could not afford it. I had faith in God and figured that something would work out. Additionally, the lady could not drive. That meant that I would have to leave my regular route to school, backtrack, and pick her up. However, the Lord knew I would make every effort for this woman. Prayerfully, I made plans for her to assist me and teach the one German class I had.

She really needed some help. Her employer had promised her that she would be able to attend English classes, that he would pay her and help her to pay taxes, and that he would give her time off and teach her to drive. None of that had happened. She wanted to make enough money so she could get her own place to live, a small apartment at least. With God's help and tender mercy, we were able to form a relationship that was mutually satisfying. I learned to look forward to picking her up in the mornings and having the short conversations in German.

I talked to her about God's plan of salvation and what He desired for her. It was very satisfying to help someone who had suffered the loss of family members and her home life in Bosnia. She missed her parents, but she could not return. As a matter of fact, she had been working with refugees from Bosnia in Germany to help them get settled, since she knew German as well as her native language. She aided the chancellor's wife with the resettlement program.

About a month later, she moved to her apartment. It was tiny, but it gave her someplace to relax and recover. The students learned to appreciate her help, as did I. I needed her, as she filled in wherever necessary in the school. She was creative and could teach art. She tie-dyed scarves and made candles.

When school closed for the summer, I was able to take her to another employer who spoke German, a manager of the Kentucky Fried Chicken restaurant located near my home. Since I knew the manager, with whom I was able to speak German, it was easy to introduce the woman, who had become my friend, to the manager. She gave her a job as soon as her application was completed. But she did not have to work there long. An accident with hot oil cut her employment short.

After a stint at a childcare agency, she learned more

English. She learned to drive and obtained a used car. From this job, she moved on to work for a Stein Mart Department Store. She became such a good employee that she now runs a division of the store. She still has an endearing accent, but her life has changed significantly. She is confident and happy. Whenever I see her, she treats me like someone of great importance. She calls me affectionately "my lady" and tells all around how she loves and appreciates me. She has given me presents that represent her gratitude. The lessons that grandmother taught me on talking about the Lord as Savior, relating to my fellow man, and being available for God to use me granted me a wonderful friend and sister in Christ.

I am grateful to the Lord for allowing me to be used in His kingdom. I am humbled by His consideration and grace toward me. It is so rewarding, and it is great godly gain for life, health, and strength.

Maternal roles that God has given me are mother to six children, grandmother to thirteen, and great-grandmother to one, at present. They are the most worthy and rewarding positions I could ever attain. With His help, I have had the rewards that my grandmother's advice, from the "shelf," has brought me. My offspring have turned out to be my best friends. As it says in Proverbs, a wise son brings joy to the heart of the parents. All six of our children have brought joy to our hearts in their continuing accomplishments. All have accepted Jesus Christ as Savior and are in their own developing walks with God. It all happened as a matter of course. The chaplain at the army base where we were living ran a revival one summer. The two eldest children decided to accept Jesus as their Savior. When the others heard the testimony, two others who did not want to be left out decided to go to the chapel the next evening with the purpose of doing the same. I was thrilled that their conversions took place so naturally and without undue pressure. My goal was to teach my family that serving the Lord is the best approach to living. I wanted them to know that they could be anything they wanted to be as Christians. Instructing them in the way I had been taught, using the Gospel and Proverbs, was the legacy I knew would be the best thing I could pass on to them. As a matter of fact, the Holy Spirit answered my prayer for guidance in teaching my children, so that I would know I had given the best instruction I could as their mother. The responsibility of preparing them for the world weighed heavy, as the time came for their going into the world fast approached. Thank the Holy Spirit, with the still small voice that was clear: "Teach them Proverbs." The successes my children have experienced are generational; they are already showing in the grandchildren. All my grandchildren have been taught about the Lord and how important it is to serve and obey Him.

The advice has served me well in my role as a mother-in-law. Although I feel I am mother to all in my family, I believe it is Jesus Christ whose love extends to everyone, and He grants it to Christians. He brings to us love that empowers. Therefore, this love requires me to treat them with the utmost respect and nurture. It requires me to respect their privacy and dignity. It permits me to share and to learn from them regarding their approach to living, their talents, and their relationship to me. I do not interfere without invitation. I do not betray confidences. This has been easy to do because they do not engage in gossip, and they are truly solicitous of each other (Grandmother's instruction in action).

I also respect them when they are at work. I do not expect them to spend a long time conversing with their mother when they are on the job. Faithfulness to God requires that a worker give an honest day's work for honest pay. Time spent away from a task is robbing an employer and is robbing God.

SELF-ASSESSMENT

Do not think too highly of yourself is another axiom
that Grandmother taught. "For everyone who exalts
himself will be humbled; and he who humbles himself
will be exalted" (Luke 18:14). In other words, we must
be wary of self-adulation when it is God who gives
us power to achieve good things in every area of our
lives. Without Him, we would be nothing. We enjoy
the very breath of life He gives. We can be happy with
what He gives, but we owe everything to Him.

LIVING BENEATH YOUR PRIVILEGE

On the other hand, as children of God, we can expect
to have all our needs met. If we first seek God and His
righteousness, all things will be added unto us. Other-
wise, we will live beneath "our privilege." This axiom
Grandmother asserted many times. He knows what
we need, and He will give us the desires of our hearts.
Seeking Him to bring about our righteous desires is
the Source to which we can go. That was evidenced in
my life when my grandmother received an inheritance
from which she gave me my first payment for college
tuition. Starting out with no visible means to study,
I now hold the doctor of philosophy, the degree the
Lord planned for me. It is in the field of linguistics,

which is the same field an intelligence test in fourth grade predicted I should study. It was the inspiration of the Holy Spirit that led to my research and the contribution to language education that resulted. It was the faith I was taught and practiced that directed my studies. Some experts in the field of neuroscience and neurolinguistics asserted that the hypotheses I used to devise a teaching model were ahead of their time. Eventual testing and research attested to the ideas God gave me.

PUTTING JESUS FIRST IN ALL THINGS

To put Jesus first in all things is a great joy because we have confidence in Him and His promises to His children to lead and guide them in the paths of righteousness for His name's sake. It is blessed assurance as it says in the hymn, "Blessed assurance, Jesus is mine." Since He never leaves or forsakes, everything done in His name will be successful, greatly successful. He promises to give us more than we can think or ask. I have learned to trust Him in everything, yes everything that concerns my children, my work, and me. I ask for His guidance to give doctors wisdom, to spend resources wisely, to go with me in travels, to grant understanding for all my students so I can teach effectively, and to live peaceably with all men.

BEWARE WHEN ALL MEN SPEAK WELL OF YOU

My grandmother taught me to beware of believing everyone's speaking well (Luke 6:26). One has to have the discernment to recognize flattery, insincere praise, false testimony, or a trap laid for downfall.

DO EVERYTHING IN DECENCY AND IN ORDER

Guided by the Holy Spirit, one can be successful in every human endeavor. It is as though a person has a teacher and a director to accompany him through life. For example, making the best presentation one can make with modest appearance and preparation opens opportunities that come in surprising ways. I still savor the meeting with the Lord Mayor of the city of Trier, Germany. I spoke in German on behalf of the Sister City of Fort Worth with my accompanying students. Later, in his office, a photograph was taken of me pretending to sign an important document while I occupied his chair. Later, the mayor and his wife arranged a visit to their home. A chauffeur picked me up in a beautiful Mercedes and took me to a beautifully appointed Kaffee Klatsch attended by friends of the mayor's wife. Because of careful attention to my wardrobe, I was prepared for the opportunity. I had a wonderful time sampling the delicacies provided by the hostess and her friends.

LIVING WELL AS UNTO THE LORD

Living well is done by living on the high road of life. This helps to avoid falling into ditches and dealing with the beggarly elements of life. That would lead to groping in the darkness. We should not participate in or condone illicit activities. Grandmother preached that we should avoid evil and the very appearance of evil. Besides, grandmother said that we crucify Jesus afresh when we choose to backslide and conduct ourselves like the unsaved. That was a caution to me.

GOD WILL MAKE A WONDER OUT OF YOU

To follow in God's paths is to be washed in the blood of the Lamb, Jesus, who will make you a beautiful, shining example to others. Grandmother was right. Everywhere we have lived, people ask me the secret of rearing a good family. I tell them that bringing up a family by the Word of God brings fulfillment (Prov. 12:20).

Putting Jesus first in all life endeavors is a guarantee for good outcomes. Grandmother said this often, "God will make a wonder out of you." This is what others have said to me in different words. Associates have asked about the secret of my parenting to produce such a family of achievement. I have replied that it was the blessing of Jesus Christ. This is the reference that came up earlier in an interview I gave, which inspired this book. The university official conducting the interview remarked that she could see the divine Hand of God running through the family's record of accomplishments, and she credited that to my grandmother, who had a love for learning and imparted that love to me.

That was revelatory, however, it was grandmother's reliance on the Lord that was the family key to success. The fact that all six of my children survived their youthful years and the serious challenges in adulthood is a marvel. Observers have mentioned, "You and your husband have had six wonderful children; none are on drugs or incarcerated." An Andrae Crouch song fits here: "This Is the Lord's Doing."

FIVE WISE AND FIVE FOOLISH VIRGINS

Another admonition Grandmother imparted was through the story of the five foolish virgins in contrast to the five wise virgins. That was a very sobering story, one that I really did not enjoy hearing because I did not know into which category I would fall. Now that

I am mature, I realize that at points in my life I fell into the category of the foolish virgins. Those are the times when I did not commit everything to the Lord through prayer and Bible reading and spoke too soon before completely understanding the origin of a problem or an event. I was cautioned to keep my lamp burning through the discipline of prayer and Bible reading.

LITTLE IS MUCH

Little is much when the Lord is in it! He will give you the desires of your heart beyond all that you can think or ask, as Grandmother taught. Both of these sayings apply to daily living and special events. My husband and I (especially myself) did not make large salaries at any point in our marriage. He was a career military officer and civil servant, and I was a substitute teacher, government teacher, regular teacher, and artist as we moved from one military post to another. In between, and during those changes of residence, I found myself in nonprofit and charitable work. With six children to rear, we were challenged economically, but we were able to provide adequately, as the Lord helped us manage to send all our kids to college. We were even able to fund a beautiful wedding in the oldest continuing military chapel in the United States at Fort Monroe. In other words, He opened doors that we could not see.

One door He opened was the opportunity to sell the art I was able to generate by word of mouth. I sold portraits and still life paintings. This was an unexpected source of income, because becoming an artist had been a long held desire of mine from elementary school. In high school, I chose art as an elective, but I did not receive a lot of encouragement for my efforts. However, one marking period my work was featured in the school hallway near the art department. It was not until I signed up for classes sponsored by the Officers Wives' Club with a reputable female artist that I realized my dream. With her encouragement, I sold everything I painted, except for the first one, which she advised me to keep so I could see my progress. She sent me to another artist from The University of Panama who instructed me in portraiture. From my latent interest in art, the Lord helped me to become an artist, helping the community of two military posts with exhibitions, demonstrations, and classes.

The other door He opened contained invitations for me to fulfill speaking engagements for young people graduating from high school. An exciting invitation gave me the opportunity to return to the church of my youth and encourage the graduates to follow the path of the Lord to become anything they aspired to become. From that event, I still get thanks from parents whose children have succeeded.

Now that our children are grown, a backward look can reveal how all this unfolded. They benefited from Grandmother's counsels, which I passed on to them: that they should do everything as unto the Lord; that they could do anything through Christ who would strengthen them; and that as much as "lieth in them," they should live peaceably with all men. As a result, they were able to contribute to their own education. Our daughter, a national merit scholar semifinalist and national achievement scholar, volunteered as a candy striper at the Gorgas Hospital, served on the Canal Zone Governor's Teen Anti-Drug Council, attended Hampton States Military Academy at West Point and other graduate schools while in the service of our country. The second son was recruited to the University of Minnesota to play football; the youngest attended Princeton as a National Merit Scholar.

Their stories continue. My daughter, who graduated from the University of Texas at Arlington, from the math and physics department, married a Dallas native in the oldest continuing chapel at Fort Monroe, Virginia, where my pastor, Bishop Strobhar officiated. That ceremony brought us another wonderful son. He had received a bachelor of arts in business administration from Texas Lutheran College. They had twin sons and a daughter. One finished with a bachelor of science in information systems, and the other attends Texas Wesleyan University preparing for a career as an officer in the National Guard. The daughter received her master's degree in speech pathology from Texas Women's University. She has honored my grandmother by including her name on every diploma that she has received. When she was born, my daughter, without coercion, gave her my grandmother's last name. That would make my grandmother happy if she were here.

Our son-in-law serves as a deacon in TD Jakes church, The Potter's House in Dallas, and my daughter serves as a member of a missionary group there. She has traveled to Mexico several times and to Budapest.

Our eldest son was responsible for conducting projects with his siblings and neighborhood children to do good deeds. One day he came to me and asked me for some little brown bags I had in my pantry. When I asked him why he needed them, he told me that his siblings and two neighbor children were collecting "glitter" to sell to the neighbors. They had formed a group called "The Helping Children" and were selling the glitter for pennies a bag. I asked him what they were telling the neighbors they were going to do with the money. I told him that they had to have a purpose. He thought for a moment and then replied they were going to help children in the hospital. I gave him the bags, and they collected what they thought was a lot money. The pennies amounted to $1.37. I wrote a check to the Rancocas Valley Hospital. The hospital administrator wrote the children a letter of thanks and invited all the children involved for a visit. This was accompanied by publicity and a picture of all the children, me, and the mother of the two girls in the group that appeared in the Burlington County Times. On the visit, they enjoyed ice cream treats. The "Helping Children" received the treats with surprise and enthusiasm. They received much more than they gave.

In Fort Bliss, he and some neighborhood children put on a Christmas pageant for the neighborhood. It was well attended by parents of approximately fifteen houses. He also spearheaded a Jerry Lewis Muscular Dystrophy Carnival behind the houses on one block. The children set up cardboard booths for entertainment. They did not make money, but they had fun. That eldest son received a presidential appointment under Ronald Reagan and went to the United States Military Academy at West Point, New York, where he was an athlete and horseman. He helped to run a Saturday night coffee house ministry for

West Point cadets and the mostly female students of King's College and surrounding communities in New York. He joined the Officers Christian Fellowship, a participating membership he continued in his adult life. He was elected as a member of the Cadet Honor Committee. He served on the honor board, a very responsible position of which elected cadets helped to administer the Honor Code during his years at the Academy. I recall a lawyer calling our home on behalf of a young man caught in cheating. My son remarked that the cadet knew the rules, and there was nothing to discuss. I remember with joy and pride as he led the Third Regiment of the "long gray line" in a march during his graduation week.

God blessed Bishop Strobhar to attend and observe the graduation activities. The minister who inspired my grandmother's life continued to serve mine as pastor at pivotal family events. While stationed near Nyack, New York, we attended his other church in Montclair, New Jersey. I was overjoyed to see him and share my joy with the pastor whose ministry had proved effective in my grandmother's life and now my own. I also praised the Lord for the respect that my son had earned at the Academy. Through my son, I was privileged to meet Christian military officers and their families in OCF, the West Point. Through him I also met General Omar Bradley, the Five-star General of World War II fame.

This son was interviewed on two television programs, NBC's *Today Show* and one on Christian Broadcasting Network, and appeared in a military magazine as the "Singing David." This was appropriate as he served as president of the West Point Glee Club and sang in the gospel ensemble. Later, he conducted subsequent tours for West Point. A plaque hangs on the wall in Thayer Hall dedicated to him. He has continued singing through the years at most of his assignments and subsequently for other community programs. The Glee Club served as ambassador to many communities in the United States. One picture of him landed in a businessman's office in Dallas. My daughter was surprised to see it when she went on assignment to that office for her company. She told me that she exclaimed, "That's my brother!"

He later married a talented classical musician, the daughter of a military chaplain and missionary. They have three children, two sons, and a daughter. He attended the Naval Postgraduate School and received a master's degree in nuclear physics. He has served as a Generals' Aide, Assistant Professor of Physics on the staff, and faculty of the United States Military Academy, Missile Battery Commander, Battalion

Commander, Brigade Commander in Iraq, Pentagon Executive Officer, and Chief of Staff of the TRDA in the Army. The tour in Iraq ended for him in certain victory. He returned from the battlefront with all of the men assigned to him at the end of their tour. He was stationed at one of Sadam Hussein's palaces at Camp Victory in Iraq, where he and the staff prayed every morning. He credited the men and especially God for this experience.

Our second son, having risen to the ranks of the USFL, CFL, and NFL, founded his own firm in Minneapolis, Minnesota. His story contains miracles that the Lord wrought in his life. Illnesses threatened his life at nineteen months and at age eleven. God preserved him to become a professional football player and a businessman. That was a normal outgrowth of his leanings. At age seven, he started a weed pulling business in our Willingboro neighborhood. Even then he was single focused. When a cousin came to see him while he was around the corner from the house, he said, "Can't you see I'm busy?" We laugh about that to this day.

He was a gifted athlete from the age of five, when he was adopted as mascot for the Hawthorne Hawks, a Little League team for which he was not allowed to play. However, he showed up at the football field at the elementary school where the games were held. They gave him the number "Double Zero" and allowed him to lead the team onto the playing field, which made him feel important when he suited up in his makeshift uniform for games. Once he sprained his thumb. His father took him to a doctor who expressed as much pride as my husband felt at his first football injury.

Later when he grew up some more, he was allowed to play football. He developed skill as a running back in Little League, junior high, and senior high in Hampton, Virginia. Though he played well for his record-holding team, my husband received orders to relocate to Fort Bliss, Texas. He played so well as a junior varsity player there, that we had to prove that the coaches did not recruit our family to move to their high school district. As one fan and friend of my husband's said, "He did everything in the games but sell popcorn in the stands."

When he was moved to the varsity level, he played well at that level, too. It was such a "high" when we saw him featured in the sports news in Sunday morning newspapers or saw him pictured on the banners of the two main city newspapers. I praised God for his physical and muscular development that had been threatened in his young life. It was proof positive that Jesus had healed him both times.

An experience that should be told about one of his healings comes to mind. Once he came to me with skin, eyes, and hands showing the yellow tint of jaundice. Quickly we got ready to go the clinic at Curundu. There, a pediatrician with a great reputation as a diagnostician examined him and took tests. After hours of waiting, an illness he had had earlier was confirmed. He called for an appointment at the Canal Zone Hospital in Ancon (Gorgas) to see an internist.

Since I thought that this was no ordinary childhood episode, I decided to go back to my house to get reinforcements. I called the neighbor next door to another Christian friend of mine who was known as a prayer warrior. After explaining the situation and my need to pray for my son with her, she came quickly. She started to pray right away, asking the Lord to heal him. This course of action taught me what to do when faced with a problem that needed God's intervention. We watched with joy as the yellow hue disappeared from his skin, his eyes, and the palms of his hands. Satisfied that the prayer had been answered, the friend left, and then my son and I left for the hospital.

When the doctor came to the examining room to see my son, I waited in anticipation to hear what he would say. I remember clearly after the examination, he said, "I don't know why your son was sent here.

I don't see any sign of illness, but I will send back my report to the doctor at the clinic." I could hardly wait to leave, to take my child home and back to his normal activities, including football.

In a follow-up visit to the clinic doctor, he expressed that he did not know what had happened. The result of his earlier examination and on-site visit confirmed his findings. Not wanting to spoil his reputation, I laughed and replied, "Doctor, you were right; I threw you a curve. I stopped at home to pray for my son before we went to see the internist."

I cannot remember his response, as it seemed to be a bit quizzical. However, my son was never sick again as a child. Later his injuries came as a result of football.

His story is stellar, as he went from trying football at age five to Little League, to junior high, senior high, college, and on to professional football. He played for three leagues: the defunct USFL, the NFL, and the CFL. His associations with athletes have brought us in contact with stars of football and baseball. He has achieved recognition in his business life as well. He recently received an honor as a Minority Business Leader of the Year in Minneapolis.

He married his college sweetheart, a talented woman who provides valued support as confidante and hostess. She is the daughter of a neonatologist and nurse practitioner. They have two children. Both of their children, having attended Christian schools for their educational foundation, are standout ice hockey players. His son attends Saint Thomas Academy in the college preparatory program, and the daughter attends Lakeville High School. They have great athletic talent. College recruiters are already observing their play on the ice. I have had the opportunity to hear the broadcasts of the boys' ice hockey games and tournaments, made possible through today's information technology.

Our third son ran track and played Little League football and lightweight college football as a quarterback. The first of his honors came when he ran in a track meet for his elementary school. With my reaction, people would have thought that he won the Olympics. He also brought us attention in junior and high school. He played trombone for the award-winning marching band of Eastwood High School. A feature article was written on him in an El Paso newspaper when his designation as a National Merit Scholar was announced. He won scholarships from the Officers Wives' Club (distaff side of the military) and ROTC.

He received his bachelor's degree from Cornell University in New York. His degree was in economics, for which he completed an honors thesis on the Canadian Railroads. After serving in the Air Force, where worked on a worldwide telecommunication system, he earned a master of business administration degree from Harvard. He worked for a while for the Burlington Northern Railroads, traveling to Swaziland twice for railroad negotiations. He served in the Air Force as an officer, working in the development of a worldwide communication system. He is now a private business consultant.

Our fourth son received his bachelor's degree from West Point, where he received an NIH scholarship for a PHD and MD. Officials at West Point told his father and me at graduation that this was a first for a cadet. While a cadet, he taught Sunday school for the West Point Chapel and participated in God's Gang, a program for youth who were the children of staff. While in graduate school at Harvard University, he taught inner-city students in Boston in math and science and also served as resident tutor at Cabot House in biology. He graduated from Harvard with the PhD and medical degrees. He was part of a special program that also incorporated studies in medical technology. He served for a while at the Bethesda Naval Hospital. He received the Fulbright Scholarship to do research in Sri Lanka after leaving the army. Today he serves as associate dean of Charles Drew Medical University in Los Angeles. He is married to another talented and

Godly woman he met at the home of missionaries. She is the daughter of evangelical Catholics. Her mother is a Bible teacher and her father, an international engineer. Her graduate degree is in urban planning. Her work today is with an agency dedicated to helping the homeless and the aged.

Our fifth son attended Princeton after high school graduation. Articles were written about him having received $800,000 in scholarship offers as the result of his research on available scholarships and grants available from organizations and corporations. The stories about him were carried in the *Dallas Morning News* and the *Fort-Worth Telegram* and on the television program *Insights*. He married his college sweetheart, the daughter of a banker and educator, and both graduated from the same class in 1995. He received a bachelor's degree in electrical and chemical engineering. He became a pilot in the U.S. Air Force. His wife, whom he married in the Princeton Chapel, received a degree in child development for which she wrote an honors thesis. They have five sons, two of which are adopted. During college they developed a desire to help children. While they attended classes, they helped tutor needy children in the Princeton area who were failing. They also developed a desire to adopt two children who were placed in the foster care system and then in an adoption agency. They are committed to helping others to adopt children.

They are doing a great job of nurturing and teaching their children about God. The family was featured in the July 2007 issue of *Redbook* in a feature titled, "Multitasking." Armed with several copies, I gave them to my dentist, who also gave me a copy from his office, my pharmacist, a friend, and family. After his graduation from the last program for the Reese Air Force Base in Lubbock, Texas, he learned to fly the B1 Bomber at Abilene, Texas. Thrilling events in which he participated encompassed his whole growing-up years. He brought honors to us in elementary school, junior high, and senior high as leader of performing groups at civic events in Fort Worth and Arlington, Texas, sports events, and as junior high class president, senior class vice-president and language club president, honor society member all four years, National Merit Scholar, Awards Day honoree, football player on a winning football team, and winner of a prestigious award given to an athlete every year. Through these activities, our family was hailed in newspapers, magazines, and television. A plaque honoring him as Mr. Lamar High School hangs in the reception area of the high school, and another hangs in the athletic department.

Two events I recall with pride and satisfaction were

the "fly-overs" he led to Arlington from Abilene for the ceremonies at the Ranger Baseball stadium. In the opening activities of each baseball season, the "Star-Spangled Banner" is played as the "Bats," as they call four B1 bombers, come roaring from the airbase in Abilene, Texas, for a patriotic display. The fly-over is timed to appear in the air over the stadium the second after the end of the "Star-Spangled Banner" ends. It was gratifying to see the planes arrive right on time, being led by my youngest child! God has given me so many wonderful experiences through this child, now a grown man. Never had I in my wildest imagination thought we would see a child flying airplanes.

His eldest son has already been written up in newspapers. He has participated as a local, regional, and state contestant in the Scripps Spelling Bee and the National Geographic Bee (geography bee). Two of the children have been designated gifted and talented. The eldest also plays the tuba, and the second son attends acting school, plays the piano, and the third plays the guitar. The first three, who are old enough to play soccer and baseball, have already won recognition. The younger two enjoy gardening and gymnastics.

Conclusion

THIS BOOK IS WRITTEN to demonstrate the faithfulness and mercy of God to His children. It is written with an attitude of gratitude for His incalculable kindness and mercies that have come to my family and me through the teachings of my grandmother. Thank God for everyone who has been gifted with a godly grandmother who gives the family the unadulterated Word of God. The unadulterated Word is life giving and rewarding because it opens the way to the treasures that God desires to give to His children, to humankind. Rearing my children has been a great blessing, and I consider it the greatest reward that the Father can give.

The book also reveals the wisdom accessible to all who read Proverbs and Ecclesiastes, as well as the Gospels. It is the study, which all who receive and accept the message of salvation, need to make a priority. It is the schooling that the novice and advanced believers need to walk with the Lord. This schooling shows the need for holiness and sanctification in which the follower of Jesus Christ separates himself from the worldly view that denigrates, destroys, and denies the power of God operating in daily life. It shows how the Christian can dedicate himself to good works and the life that can rest in Him and receive all God has promised to give him. It inspires the ongoing development in the Christian life. In sum, it is the surety for a good life and the life hereafter. The Word of God will not return void. It will accomplish the purposes for which it was sent.

Therefore, it does not matter where the children of God should worship. It does not matter about denomination. It matters only that the unadulterated Word of God is presented. It is effective in feeding and nurturing the man's spirit when it has made true repentance and received the gifts and the bounties of salvation. I have worshiped in Pentecostal, Nazarene, Baptist, Methodist, Disciples of Christ, Lutheran, Presbyterian, and Catholic congregations. In all of them, I have received blessings.

My dear grandmother would be glad that I remembered her practical presentations of the Lord and His ways in preparation for meeting any situation or task we face in life. As she said so many times, "I tried Him and I know Him." He can supply all my needs according to His riches in Glory. To live otherwise would have been living beneath my "privilege," as Grandmother said, "For God delights in giving good gifts to His children." Now that I've gone to Grandmother's shelf, I can say the same. I've tried Him and I know Him.

It will be a great time when the prayer that Jesus prayed comes true: "I would that they all become one." What a glorious day that will be.

Thank You, Jesus!

Thank you for giving me a godly grandmother!

About the Author

$\mathcal{B}$ERNICE REID IS AN award-winning educator, artist, journalist, and musician whose career has spanned more than fifty years. Currently she teaches online internationally. She is a member and past president of the National League of American Pen Women Inc., a professional organization of writers, artists, and composers. She holds a bachelor of education degree, cum laude, from West Virginia State University, a master's degree and a doctorate in humanities from the University of Texas at Arlington, with a concentration in second language acquisition. She holds certifications in the study of English, French, German, and Social Studies. She also holds certificates in Christian Education and Administration from Pensacola Christian College, School of Tomorrow, Dominion Christian Center, and a certificate of ordination from Faith Temple, United Holy Church in Chester, Pennsylvania.

With two other teachers and a counselor, she founded the Arlington Cultural and Educational

Foundation with a grant from a local Domino's franchise. Its endeavors to enrich the lives of students were supported by the Center for Minority Culture at the University of Texas at Arlington. This expanded to include Trinity Lyceum, a school with an individualized and accelerated Christian education.

Her honors and associations include Sharon Christa McAuliffe Education Flag of Learning and Liberty; Wall of Fame—Arlington Independent School District; Two Duden Awards—Outstanding Teacher of German—Duden Publishers and Brockhaus AG, Mannheim, Germany, and American Association Teachers of German, Cherry Hill, NJ; Outstanding Teacher in the Southwest; Thanks to Teacher Award—Apple Computer; Junior League of Dallas; KVTV; National Alliance of Business; NCNB; Arlington Will Award and Recognize Excellence; AWARE Foundation; and AISD.

Dr. Reid is listed in the *Cambridge Who's Who; The World Who's Who of Women; Notable Women of Texas; Dictionary of Biography; Personalities of the South*; and *Who's Who Among Students in Colleges and Universities.*

Other memberships include: Modern Language Association; Alpha Kappa Mu, National Scholastic Honorary Society; Alpha Chi, National Foreign

Language Society; and Pi Delta Phi National French Honorary Society.

She was inspired to write *Grandmother's Shelf* to portray the loving, teaching of faith from her grandmother and as testimony to Jesus Christ's salvation, redemption, and restoration. She hopes this book will minister to all who will read it, especially young people.

This the first time Dr. Reid has written for the public at large. In the past, her writings were academic and journalistic. As a matter of fact, she was named editor emeritus of her college newspaper, the *Yellow Jacket* in 1957. Since then, she has served as a public relations representative, freelance writer, and publisher of some in-house newspapers and magazines.

Her other books are: *The Semiotics of the Russian Icon Compared to Those of Beckett's Tableau* and *Second Language Acquisition Based on Neurolinguistics, Psycholinguistics, and Applied Linguistic Theory.*

Dr. Reid is married to Carlton Reid, retired military officer, retired regional director of Headstart and accountant. Together they have been blessed with six adult children, thirteen grandchildren, and one great-grandchild.

To Contact the Author

trinitylyceum@yahoo.com